GOVERNMENT REGULATION: WHAT KIND OF REFORM?

Eileen Shanahan, *Moderator*

Hubert H. Humphrey
Ronald Reagan
Hendrik Houthakker
Ralph Nader

A Round Table held on 11 September 1975
and sponsored by the
American Enterprise Institute for Public Policy Research
and the
Hoover Institution on War, Revolution and Peace

ISBN 0-8447-2070-4
LIBRARY OF CONGRESS CATALOG CARD NUMBER 76-321

PRINTED IN UNITED STATES OF AMERICA

EILEEN SHANAHAN, Washington Bureau of the *New York Times,* and moderator of the discussion: Tonight we are going to discuss a subject that has increasingly occupied the attention of many people who are concerned about the proper role of government, about the functioning of the American economy, and about how each of these could be improved.

Government regulation of business in the United States is old. Its history goes back almost a hundred years to the creation of the Interstate Commerce Commission to deal with some very real ills of the last century. One of those ills was that railroads serving monopoly routes would frequently, in fact generally, jack up the rates during harvest time when the farmers had no alternative but to submit.

But that is ancient history. The questions before the panel tonight are these: Is the regulation that began then and is now implemented by six major government agencies and offices within many others—is that regulation still justified? Is it wise? Does it cost too much? All of these questions are receiving increasing scrutiny. President Ford has let it be known that getting rid of some government regulation is one of the major issues on which he will run for election in his own right in 1976. He is for decreasing and even eliminating much existing regulation, but there are those who hold a different view.

I want to start with Ralph Nader who has taken the position that there are really two different kinds of regulation and that we must distinguish very carefully between them before deciding, or trying to decide, what to keep and what not to keep.

1

RALPH NADER, Center for Study of Responsive Law: I think it is useful to frame the discussion with this distinction in mind: there is health and safety regulation, which deals with such matters as drugs or food or automobiles, and there is economic regulation, which deals with the setting of rates or the operation of certain procedures in a given industry.

Of these, the former, health and safety regulation, tends to involve serious human values, such as the security of life and limb, and it is also the less susceptible to market support precisely because of the dangers latent in automobiles and nuclear power plants and drugs.

The second kind of regulation, economic regulation, has been brought about by a variety of factors. One of these is economic crisis such as the sharp inflationary spiral which led to the creation of the wage-price agencies a few years ago. Another is a less-than-competitive structure in an industry, for example, the natural gas industry. And a third—historically the most common cause of economic regulation, surprising as it may seem—is the desire of the industries themselves. The truck companies and the airlines, for example, crave regulation by government agencies that will fix their prices at higher-than-competitive levels.

I think it is important to look at regulation issues in terms of the human needs of society, so that we don't deal in easy slogans and easy scenarios. Instead we should ask ourselves what human purpose regulation fulfills, whether it is just or unjust, whether it is adequate or inadequate, and finally whether there might be a better way to improve economic performance, either by more competition, more consumer cooperatives, or more public enterprise.

MS. SHANAHAN: Professor Houthakker, do you agree with some or all of what Ralph Nader has said?

HENDRIK HOUTHAKKER, Department of Economics, Harvard University: I think that Mr. Nader has made a very important distinction between different types of regulation. Certainly, we don't want to treat health and safety on quite the same level as economic efficiency. Indeed, I might add environmental factors to Mr. Nader's list of causes of regulation, for to some extent they also justify a degree of regulation that is not justified strictly on economic grounds.

However, I may perhaps make one qualification: regulation is not automatically good merely because it is intended to protect health, safety, or the environment. These considerations are sometimes used to mask much less desirable ends. I would insist on differentiating between intent and effect. Health regulations, for instance, have an economic aspect: we have to consider whether particular health regulations really are worth their cost. But having added that qualification, I think the distinction drawn by Ralph Nader is a very important one.

MS. SHANAHAN: Governor Ronald Reagan, what do you say to this introductory point?

RONALD REAGAN, former governor of California: I can't quarrel with anything that has been said so far, but at the same time I have to say that, while this may sound simplistic, I believe that government's principal function is to protect us from each other, not from ourselves. We get onto dangerous ground when we allow government to decide what is good for us. I could give an example of that in the field of health and safety regulations.

Right now the motorcycle riders are all protesting that the federal government wants to force them to wear helmets. This issue first confronted me as governor of California when the federal government threatened to shut off federal highway funds if we didn't enforce helmet-wearing with legislation. I said I would join any propaganda or public relations campaign to urge motorcyclists to wear helmets—since I happen to think anyone is foolish to ride a motorcycle at all and very foolish to do so without a helmet. But I don't think government has any business telling a person he has to wear a helmet. I'm all for the government's inspecting motorcycles for brakes and lights and anything that prevents them from coming across the center line and endangering me or anyone else. But a person who wants to ride a motorcycle without a helmet is

3

only endangering himself, and I don't think it is any of government's business.

Both in the field of health and in the economic field, government has grown to such an extent that I'm afraid it is showing a lack of respect for the average citizen. With government fostering the idea that the citizen can't even buy a box of Post Toasties for himself without being cheated, one wonders how voters are supposed to be able to pick people for government who are wise enough to make all these decisions? When government starts showing a lack of respect for the people, the people start showing a lack of respect for government.

I don't believe the average citizen has any idea how complex his government has become. He can't conceive of the fact that there are eighty-nine agencies regulating the petroleum industry and that not even the Office of Management and Budget knows how many agencies and boards and commissions and so forth there are, many of which conflict with each other.

Just recently the Department of HEW went into a hospital in Ohio and said the plastic liners had to be taken out of the waste baskets because if one of them caught fire the noxious fumes would be injurious to the patients. But the plastic liners had only been used because the Occupational Health and Safety Administration had said they were necessary to protect the employees of the hospital from contamination in handling the waste in the waste baskets. The only thing I figure the hospital can do is put a guard on the steps to scout ahead and see which agency is coming to inspect it next.

MR. NADER: Of course, if a motorcycle operator who is not wearing a helmet is in an accident and is sprawled on the highway, you could expect a police car, taxpayer-paid, to rush to the scene, and an ambulance, taxpayer-paid, to drive the victim to a taxpayer-paid hospital; and you could expect the risk of secondary accidents to increase with the motorcycle driver sprawled on the highway unconscious—which he wouldn't be if he were wearing a motorcycle helmet.

It isn't that simple. If you are on your own private

road on your farm and you don't want to wear a motorcycle helmet, fine, I agree with you. But when you are on a public highway, you are endangering people if you cannot escape from a spill, and you may have to burden the taxpayer with picking you up and taking you to a tax-financed institution to care for you. That's the real problem. Would you favor the abolition of all victimless crime penalties, all legal attempts to prevent people from harming themselves?

MR. REAGAN: I find it very hard to determine what exactly victimless crimes are—and I realize there is a gray area in all of these things. But I do think you have described an area of very light gray.

MR. NADER: Well, define it yourself.

MR. REAGAN: If a man falls off that motorcycle speeding down the highway, chances are he is going to be somewhat disabled and will end up lying on the highway with or without the helmet. [Laughter.]

MR. NADER: That's not true. As a matter of fact, the studies have shown that the greatest single saver of motorcyclists' lives is the helmet, and studies have also shown—I'm sure you've read about them in California—that the chain-type accident occurs where an obstruction on the highway causes a whole stream of accidents.

As I say, I agree with you that ideally helmets should be a voluntary measure, but when motorcyclists are on public highways and are burdening the public in terms of secondary accidents and death and injury, I think one can legitimately say that using a helmet is a very small price to pay.

MR. REAGAN: But how far does government go in trying to make life totally accident-free? Do we stand guard at the beach and tell the surf rider when we think the surf is too dangerous? Do we tell the mountain climber he can't climb the mountain? After all, rescue teams may have to help him also at the taxpayer's expense. Where do we draw

5

the line? One government agency has issued a warning to mothers that sharp, shiny scissors can cause howls of pain from small school-aged children. Well, I think dull, rusty ones can too, but I don't think we are going to do away with scissors. [Laughter.]

PROFESSOR HOUTHAKKER: Well, to some extent the public itself draws this line. Recently, a requirement for seat belts in every car was put through and it turned out to be so unpopular that now belts are no longer mandatory, or maybe the buzzer mechanism was taken out—I'm not quite sure. Some people may have realized that seat belts did improve the safety of cars. Nevertheless, the public evidently felt that this was going too far, that the regulation wasn't worth the trouble.

MR. NADER: Of course, there are a lot of areas of health and safety regulation that are much more serious than the examples you are giving.

MR. REAGAN: Yes.

MR. NADER: For example, 15,000 diabetics are dying every year as a result of the adverse effects of drugs taken for their diabetic condition, and the drug companies did not warn them of these adverse effects even though the companies were aware of them. There are flammable fabrics burning people, children, to death. There are very hazardous products on the market. It is easy to give absurd examples, but the serious question, which you asked earlier in the program, is, Do the people have an opportunity to decide what government is going to do for them or by them or to them? I don't think these regulatory agencies are open enough to the people to allow that kind of participation.

MR. REAGAN: Well, but for every case you can bring up of a drug that slipped by the Food and Drug Administration and has been harmful to some people, you can bring up dozens of cases of the Food and Drug Administration going too far. The Food and Drug Administration in recent years has gone so far that it has cut in half, more than in half, the production of new medicines and drugs in America. We no longer lead the world as we did, and we've added hundreds of millions of dollars to the cost of the drugs that the people must buy. Where a leading drug company a few years ago only had to submit about seventy-odd pages of data to support a license application, it now has to send 73,000 such pages. And cases can be made for the thousands and thousands of people who have died or suffered in this country because drugs used in other countries, that have been passed there and proven effective in the market, have been denied them. I think something more than 40,000 tuberculars alone have died in this country who conceivably could have been saved by a drug that has been used widely in the last few years throughout Europe.

MR. NADER: I don't think there is any evidence to support that at all. I think that is part of the propaganda that has been put forward about the Food and Drug Administration.

As you know, there are too many useless drugs in the marketplace. The National Academy of Sciences documents this. Many of these drugs should be taken off the market. I think if you read the Senate Small Business Committee study of the assertions you are making, you'll see that they simply are not supported by the evidence. What we do know is that fortunately our Food and Drug Administration stopped the drug Thalidomide, which caused 10,000 deformed births in Western Europe and Japan, from coming into this country.

I really think that what we have to ask ourselves in this discussion is, To what extent can these agencies reflect the value system of a population by operating openly, accountably, and subject to citizen or consumer participation? Right now it is big business and the lawyers of big business that have access to these agencies and it is very difficult for the public to find out what they are paying for or what they are being exposed to as a result of the behavior of these agencies.

PROFESSOR HOUTHAKKER: I think we can agree that to a large extent the agencies frequently have become much too responsive to the industries they are supposed to control. In fact, in many cases it can be shown that the agencies were created because the industries wanted them, as I think you already mentioned, and increasing the distance between the two is one reform that would bring about some progress. But there is still the wider question of whether we need that much regulation at all. I'm now thinking particularly of what you earlier called economic regulation as distinct from health and safety.

Opening up these agencies will do some good, but that approach still leaves us with the problem that expertise in these industries is naturally concentrated in the industries themselves. Anybody who knows a lot about the petroleum industry is very likely to be employed in the petroleum industry, and that may bias his judgment no matter how good his intentions are. That is why I think there is, just from the point of view of an operating democracy, a good case for not inserting the government into areas where expertise is concentrated in the hands of people who also have a direct interest in the outcome of government action. Instead, we should leave the government as much as possible out of the economic field.

MR. NADER: If there is a competitive market structure.

PROFESSOR HOUTHAKKER: I agree with that. Competition is something which I think the government should develop and foster by all legitimate means. There are some areas where competition cannot be created, and those I would certainly agree need regulation. There are also areas where competition could exist but is being deliberately suppressed.

MS. SHANAHAN: You mentioned that expertise generally is to be found chiefly within an industry. I think the proponents of a consumer advocacy agency, of whom we have one of the leaders right here, have suggested that one of the purposes of such an agency would be to develop just such expertise. Are you completely skeptical about the actual possibility of that?

PROFESSOR HOUTHAKKER: I am. I wouldn't say it is impossible, but I think it is difficult and expensive and unlikely. Instead, I would like to see the government withdraw as much as possible from detailed regulation and not go into areas where highly specific expertise is needed.

Now, there are undoubtedly cases where this is not desirable. It's clearly not possible to leave drug regulation entirely to the industry, even though I think we may be doing too much. In those areas, it may be possible to find people who know. But there are all the other areas. Just today Mr. Gary Seevers, who is now a member of the Commodity Futures Trading Commission, was saying that there are really very, very few people outside the industry who really know what commodity futures trading is all about—because if they are good at it, they go into the industry.

MS. SHANAHAN: But how can an agency regulate intelligently if its only source of information is the very people who have a vested interest in a particular outcome of that agency's decision?

PROFESSOR HOUTHAKKER: When I was in the government, I was struck by the fact that our information on petroleum seemed to come almost entirely from one company which I will not name because this is not an occasion for commercials—

MR. NADER: I don't think that would be a commercial. It would be just the opposite.

PROFESSOR HOUTHAKKER: No, because the company's people did a good job. Not only did they give us informative answers, but they also seemed to anticipate what questions might come up and by the time we asked they had already done the necessary studies. [Laughter.] Just from the point of view of advice they did a very good job. Nevertheless, there was always the nagging feeling that perhaps some company interest would also be represented in what they told us. That I thought was a very unhealthy situation, and I don't really know how you can avoid it if you want to control an industry in any detail.

MR. NADER: Of course, I think the evidence is quite clear here. The Interstate Commerce Commission (ICC) is supposed to regulate the railroads, and the railroads never have told the Interstate Commerce Commission who owns the railroads. The Civil Aeronautics Board (CAB) is supposed to regulate the airlines and it still hasn't found out who owns the airlines. And to this day the various energy agencies do not have independently verified information on oil reserves, gas reserves, and many of the pricing systems between the various parts of the oil industry.

I think that one needs to be very skeptical about experts who have higher allegiances than their expertise. Experts who work for corporations or for other vested interest groups often inject the corporate value system into their assessments, by either keeping some information secret or emphasizing other information which isn't as relevant. You know, there were experts on Vietnam in the Defense Department and State Department. The fate of experts who have a higher allegiance than their own knowledge and conscience is quite apparent as far as the public results are concerned.

MS. SHANAHAN: Do you have a proposal for dealing with that problem?

MR. NADER: Actually, there are many proposals. We want to avoid thinking there is just one solution. We need to open up these agencies to freedom of information. We need citizen action rights to sue these agencies. If a government bureaucrat's power is totally secure, he is not going to be responsive. It is only when it is insecure, when that power can be challenged either in court or in other forums, that he becomes responsive. We need to give the people who represent large groups, whether they be minority groups or the poor or consumers or the small taxpayer, the wherewithal—and by that I mean the funds—to get their own specialists and their own lawyers to participate in all these regulatory agencies, whether concerned with crooked advertising or natural gas prices or what have you.

That is why I think the consumer advocacy agency is so important. It doesn't regulate. It's a bureaucracy fighter. It's an inflation fighter. It's an injector of deliberate, skilled information representing a variety of interests that are now not represented, and also advocating procedures to make regulation more fair. I dare say that your theories on deregulation would have attained recognition in government far earlier if there had been an agency that could advocate them in the hearings and all the other processes of the regulatory agencies. Instead, we lost ten, fifteen, twenty years before we came around to this conclusion. Now, both liberals and conservatives think that the CAB's rate-setting function should be abolished and that the ICC's rate setting for truck companies should be abolished because they just keep prices high for consumers.

MR. REAGAN: I want to reply; but first I'd like to go back to the drug situation for a moment—merely to say that I reject your suggestion that my facts weren't verifiable. I think they are.

On the ICC, though, as long as I can remember, the railroads have protested regulations which they said were making it impossible for them to be economical and to run the railroads the way they should, and they have asked for release from many of these. I've been told that something like 42 trillion rate decisions were given by the ICC in its eighty-five-year history and that they are not even indexed. In the end the federal government had to take over most of the passenger traffic, and the first thing the federal government did was free itself from having to observe the ICC regulations.

I couldn't agree more with the criticism of the power of bureaucrats. It is the only time under our Constitution that when we are charged with something, we are therefore automatically guilty as charged. If we break a law or commit murder, we're presumed innocent unless and until proven guilty, but if a bureaucrat comes in from one of the agencies and says we've broken one of his regulations, that bureaucrat is judge, jury, and executioner and we have to take *him* to court.

Recently, three salt companies concluded a case. They were charged with violating regulations. They were taken to court and they decided to fight it. Had they not fought it, the fine would have been $150,000. Two-and-a-half years later a federal jury found them innocent and, by then, they had spent $775,000.

The paperwork alone required by government is staggering. It is estimated that small businessmen in America spend a total of 130 million man-hours a year filling out government-required forms, which adds about $50 billion a year to the cost of doing business. Now, the consumer pays the cost, because it is a business expense. But then we pay about another $20 billion in taxes so someone in Washington can handle all that paper. In spite of all of the talk in Washington about improving this situation, this year it is estimated that the small businessman will have to do 20 percent more paperwork than last year. I don't think anyone recognizes the extent to which small businesses are regulated.

I agree with you that business is responsible in part for going along with regulations that finally have brought it some advantages, such as preventing entry of new competition into the field, price fixing, and so forth. I still think that kind of thing is wrong. And I think regulation has led to what I call an interlocking bureaucracy. The bureaucracy in government is now being matched by a bureaucracy employed by business to do business with the bureaucracy here. The two bureaucracies are feeding on each other and neither one of them wants the other to go away because then it wouldn't have a job.

MR. NADER: If you make that your campaign theme next year, you'll be making a major contribution to the American dialogue—if you speak out against corporate socialism, government subsidies of big business, corporations that are so big they can't be allowed to fail so only small businesses can go bankrupt. A company that is big, like Lockheed and those other giants, can go to Washington instead of going out of business. And you are absolutely right that in that situation there is a massive outflow of the taxpayers' revenue into the coffers of the giant corporations. It certainly doesn't make them more efficient—any more than welfare creates an incentive to work. That's what the corporations seem to reflect.

And above all, what really must be emphasized is that people who say they are conservatives do not speak out enough against monopolistic practices, against highly concentrated industry. They don't speak for the enforcement of the antitrust laws, for beefing up the Justice Department's budget. They don't speak out against the massive inflated contracts and subsidies that pour out of Washington which make up the bulk of government expenditures. It isn't the regulatory agencies that make up the bulk of government. Their total budgets are less than three-quarters of $1 billion out of a $350 billion budget. It is all these giant agencies who are accounts receivables for these giant industries.

I think if you focus on that, you'll see that our democracy is going down the drain, because when Westinghouse can't sell its nuclear plants, it asks Mr. Frank Zarb [administrator of the Federal Energy Administration] to buy them. That's "lemon socialism." If a plant is a lemon, sell it to the government the way Consolidated Edison sold out to the government of New York State. If you speak out against that, politics will be enriched.

MR. REAGAN: Mr. Nader, I've been speaking out against that for a long time.

MR. NADER: The press isn't covering you.

MR. REAGAN: I know it. [Applause.] I'm labeled, so they're not covering me.

MS. SHANAHAN: Let me raise a specific question in this area. You mentioned earlier, Governor Reagan, that eighty-nine different agencies regulate the petroleum industry. To be so high, I think that figure must include all the industry advisory committees, and these are committees that business has insisted upon as channels for its own input. I think that's correct, and I think procedures initiated by business also account for a lot of the man-hours and pieces of paper you cited.

Especially since we have this marvelous agreement about the pernicious effect of excessive bureaucracy, I'm wondering what thoughts you have as to how to reduce the proliferation of paperwork that occurs not just because some liberals or radicals want regulation, but because business insists on detailed safeguards, multiple duplicating inputs into the process, and so on.

MR. REAGAN: Oh, no. The 130 million man-hours I mentioned only applied to small businessmen, not the big corporations. I'm talking about the druggist who says it takes more time to fill out the form for the government than it does to mix the prescription. I'm talking about any number of small merchants who are harassed by regulations, and the estimated amount of paper they use is 10 billion pieces a year. I haven't worked it out, but I have been told that the amount of paper sent by business to Washington at Washington's demand would fill fifty baseball stadiums from the dugout to the top row of the stadium.

MS. SHANAHAN: Let me get at the question a different way. You raised a point, which Ralph Nader enthusiastically endorsed, about the vested interest that business has built up in regulation. I think most of the panel and many members of the audience are aware that the first President to propose getting the government out of regulation of transportation was Dwight Eisenhower. How many years ago was that? But it doesn't happen. As someone who covers the Congress, I believe that one of the reasons it doesn't happen is that business is overtly or not so overtly lobbying against deregulation. Do you agree? And if so, how do we as a society cope with the fact that business, many businesses, small and large (trucking companies are mostly small businesses and they're among the ones who do), continue to lobby for regulation? How do we cope with that?

MR. REAGAN: Well, for one thing, even though Mr. Nader

hasn't been hearing me, I've been addressing business groups and asking them if they believe in free enterprise —because I believe that we should return as much as possible to the marketplace. Going back to my statement about government protecting us from each other—yes, I want the government to make sure that the airplane I get on is as safe as it reasonably can be, that standards are established for safety. I am proud of the fact that the safest ship you can be on is an American ship because no other country in the world has the safety requirements that we do. All that I believe in. I believe in pure food and drug inspection to make sure that the kind of problem that caused the Food and Drug Administration and the Pure Food Act in the first place—poisoned meat in a store—doesn't recur.

But businesses, of course, have found that the cocoon can be very warm and comfortable, so they go along and put up with the harassment. At the large corporation level, with their computerized operations and accountants, the paperwork isn't the burden that it is to the smaller businessman.

I think all of us have got to ask ourselves very quickly how much farther we can go down this road, because we know already that government is taking virtually half of every dollar earned in the United States. And beyond that, there is a hidden tax that we don't even see. I'm very embarrassed to say this in the presence of the professor, but I received a degree in economics—I think it was an honorary degree. [Laughter.]

PROFESSOR HOUTHAKKER: It was deserved anyway.

MR. REAGAN: Well, I think that the cost of these regulations, which is passed on from business to the customer, in a way is another tax that we don't see. I'd like to know how much the cost imposed by government for all of this regulation to supposedly protect us contributes to inflation.

Then, too, businesses can be damaged by regulation, with no redress from government. We hear all about what business can take from government in the form of the so-called subsidy, but it can also lose. There is the case of the businessman whose toy the products safety administration decided might be dangerous to children. He followed its recommendations about what he should do in making the toy safe. But somehow the agency made a mistake and withdrew the toy from the market after he had invested all his money in changing the entire product. There is no provision in government for any repayment to him and he is virtually bankrupt.

MR. NADER: Nor is there any provision in government for compensation to the victims of dangerous toys. That's where I would have my priority. If the government makes a mistake in dealing with a small business, it should make amends. But I would really highlight the victims—the children who have been burned to death or maimed seriously. What is the government going to do for the children or their families?

MR. REAGAN: I'm not a lawyer, but aren't you getting into the area of civil suit and redress for selling a product that causes harm?

MR. NADER: When the government refuses to enforce the law that protects children from being maimed by a dangerous product, it is the same as the government acting wrongly and injuring a small business. Why all the concern for the business side? It is nice to be concerned about small business. You said there are 130 million man-hours of paperwork every year—

MR. REAGAN: But I'm concerned as a consumer—

MR. NADER: —and there are 20 million businesses so they must spend about six hours a year each on paperwork. That's pretty heavy. [Laughter.]
I'm concerned about the children. If concern starts with the victims and works backward, the priorities will be in order. If it starts with the people who have got the wealth and the power and works down to the victim, the priorities can start shooting off in wayward directions.

MR. REAGAN: I think our priorities were in order in California. We started the first real consumer protection agency in the United States in California during my administration. We did all the things you're talking about.

MR. NADER: What was the budget?

MR. REAGAN: I can't recall the exact budget, but I can tell you that we did all the things—furniture, clothing, all of these. I've gone through and seen the agency performing tests on upholstery, both items imported from overseas and those manufactured in this country. We set up a provision whereby anyone with a complaint about a mechanic cheating him on his car could call a certain number and get the help of the protection agency.

But we found out something else interesting. First of all, we found out there wasn't as much shoddy produce in America as we had been led to believe. It was very seldom that we discovered serious violations. We also found that in over 90 percent of the cases that came to our department, we were able to resolve them between the complainant and the business, and we found that businesses were most anxious to resolve the issue. I don't think the average businessman is out to cheat anyone. Only a very few times did government have to bring pressure to bear to get justice for the consumer.

But don't say that I'm just on the side of business. I'm on the side of a society that today rides on government-regulated transportation, including everything from taxicabs to airplanes. Everything we produce is shipped on government channels, even down to pipelines. We read by government-regulated light. We heat by government-regulated gas. We are the most regulated society in the world, and we are paying for it not only in coin of the realm, but also in a greater loss of freedom than any of us realize. We have moved a great distance from the system that originated in this country, a system that was based on the ultimate in individual freedom consistent with an orderly society.

MR. NADER: Of course, I hope you agree that a lot of this government regulation is corporate regulation one step removed. I'm sure the millions of Americans who are paying skyrocketing electric bills and gas and gasoline bills and telephone bills are not enthralled by the state utility commissions that supposedly regulate the utilities in their interest.

Let me put it this way: Would you make a list of all the subsidies that government gives to business and then specify whether or not you are opposed to each? Would you focus on that issue, because subsidies are such a large part of the so-called government involvement in business? Subsidies are just a slush fund. Uncle Sam is a sugar daddy for the big corporations. Big business couldn't exist without big government.

MR. REAGAN: Professor, would you take that on for me?

PROFESSOR HOUTHAKKER: I will take that on. [Laughter.]

MR. NADER: Would you make a list of the subsidies? You said you are against subsidies. Would you make a list and let the American people know which ones you are against because your word carries weight?

PROFESSOR HOUTHAKKER: I'm sure that Governor Reagan could do a very useful job on this. Let me just say, though, that it is not, I think, generally true that all of government's involvement is at the behest of big business only. I think small business also plays a very important role. As Ms. Shanahan has already mentioned, in the case of trucking, for instance, it isn't really big business that is involved.

I would like to come back for a moment to the very important questions she raised: Why is it that business is supporting regulation and why is it that the Eisenhower effort and the Kennedy effort and the Nixon effort and now, of course, the Ford effort at deregulation have all met with difficulty? Maybe this time the climate is better than it was, in part because all the previous efforts may now be bearing some fruit. But the question is, why is business supporting regulation to some extent?

I was involved in the effort to deregulate surface transportation in 1971 and was somewhat acquainted with the aftermath in Congress. As we have already seen, there is a separate bureaucracy in business which doesn't consist of business firms but of trade associations. Their main role is to maintain contact with the government to further the interest of their industry as they see it. Very often they don't really represent their members all that well.

I have long come to the conclusion that people from trade associations, however bright and well-informed they are, give you the party line. When we drew up the railroad deregulation bill of 1971, for instance, we had conversations with truckers, individually. If you want to know something about an industry, talk with the people who actually run the industry, individually, and you will often get a very different story. One trucking executive whom I remember very vividly told me that his firm had a subsidiary in the Canadian province of Alberta. It had acquired this subsidiary because of some claim it had on the company, and management thought, "Well, we have to sell this right away because there is no regulation of trucking in Alberta and we can't live in such an environment." After a while they found that they could very well make money without regulation. This particular man told me and my associates that he could perfectly well live with deregulation but there were other people in the industry who wouldn't. Well, the trade associations generally speak for this minority or majority of firms that believe that maybe they can live with it but somebody else can't.

One of the most serious problems we face in working toward reform is the loyalty that exists in many industries to the industry itself. When you talk with steel people—I have met a great many of them, and they are very fine people, some of them good businessmen, others not so good, but, nevertheless, they run their own businesses—what strikes you is that they talk all the time about the steel industry.

As an economist I wouldn't mind in the least hearing a businessman talk about what is good for his company. That is what a businessman is for. And I wouldn't mind at all, as an American citizen, to hear that something is good for the United States. But when I hear them say that such and such is good for the steel industry or for the oil industry or for the cement industry, I become a little worried, because I cannot recognize the steel industry or any other industry as a legitimate object of loyalty.

What this really means is that there is a certain competitive structure in this industry which is sustained by government measures, and that bothers me. I would be much happier if the role of trade associations were somewhat smaller, and I say this in the knowledge that Washington is the home of many trade associations—of which there are probably a few representatives here in the audience. But I think this is an aspect of the situation that doesn't always get sufficient emphasis. It is also one of the reasons why I don't think that the giant corporations are as big a part of the problem as you think they are. I'm not saying that they are completely without blame. They play the game, too. But in my experience much of the problem is with smaller firms that feel they can't stand the competition and therefore rely on government.

MR. NADER: List of subsidies? [Laughter.]

MR. REAGAN: Well, we've dwelt on business a lot and I realize now I'm going to step on sacred soil, so I'll preface my remarks by saying that I'm a lifetime union member and was six times president of my union.

But what about the Jones law? This is the act requiring that products moving between American ports be shipped in American bottoms, with American crews. Now, this is a labor law. This was lobbied through at the behest of labor.

MS. SHANAHAN: The purpose of which, as initially stated anyway, was to retain a vigorous merchant marine—

MR. REAGAN: That's right.

MS. SHANAHAN: —which we might need in time of war as well as for peacetime purposes.

MR. REAGAN: And you've guessed already what I'm getting at. So many subsidies, outright subsidies, started with the idea of what this country had to preserve in case of war. I don't know whether this is still necessary, with modern technology, but when I was much younger, this country subsidized watchmaking because the watchmakers' skills were very useful in the fusing of artillery shells and so forth—and because we had to subsidize to compete with the great watch industry in Switzerland. We subsidized this business only to have those skills here in case of need, in case we had no access to Switzerland. The same is true of the Jones Act. This was lobbied through on the grounds that if we let the rest of the world carry our produce, we would have no ships in time of war.

But here are Swedish bottoms taking liquefied natural gas from Alaska to Japan in such quantity that they literally fuel the utilities industry of Japan, while parts of the U.S. East Coast, which are so dependent on oil, may be faced with a shortage this winter. But Swedish ships cannot carry that gas through the canal to New Hampshire where it is so much needed because they cannot travel from an American port to an American port.

U.S. shipping cannot compete with foreign rates and wages. The ships must be both built in America and manned by American crews. Here we are in another gray area. Do we find some way to restore coast-wide shipping in America, which we no longer have to any extent at all, or can we afford to eliminate the American merchant marine because of this competitive pricing situation and then face the risk of having to start from scratch in wartime? I don't know the answer to that dilemma or to those posed by many other subsidies.

I want to associate myself with the viewpoint that not just big business asks for protective regulation. I had my brains kicked in while I was governor because I wouldn't go along with a law in California that would have allowed the peach growers to shut out any hobby farmers that wanted to raise peaches on fourteen or fifteen acres, and they are back at it again.

We have the dairymen. They are in the government subsidy cocoon, and if you want to get in a big fight, try to tell them that you want them to get back out on free

21

enterprise and sell the milk, and the one that can sell it for the least, let him do it. They want that minimum protection, which means that you are subsidizing the most inefficient so that they can't be driven out of business by the more efficient.

MS. SHANAHAN: We're getting to an area of agreement here on the Jones Act. When President Ford had his economic summit meetings a year ago there were some votes taken among, I think it was, twenty-two famous economists who covered almost the entire spectrum from left to right. I believe the Jones Act was one of the issues on which they were unanimous, that this ban on foreign shipping between U.S. coastal points adds I forget how much to consumer prices and ought to be abolished.

I'm not sure when it was that I first heard that claim, but I think it might have been in the early or middle 1950s. You haven't said so, but I think you would certainly agree with me—Dr. Houthakker, too—that the Jones Act would be a good thing to get rid of. What would you say from your different perspectives, backgrounds, and, if I may say, different functions in society, that is, different occupations, about how we could go about getting rid of the Jones Act? Let's concentrate on the Jones Act as one example of government regulation that burdens the U.S. consumer with higher prices. Or is there some other item that you would all agree we should get rid of—perhaps the detailed regulation of trucks? You have to file a tariff, a rate, specifying intent to ship a certain chemical, named by name, from Kansas City to Chicago—it is literally as detailed as that. There is very widespread agreement among people in this field that we ought to get rid of this requirement.

How do we go about it?

MR. NADER: By making the consumer the measure of the policy. The economy exists for the consumer's well being. Adam Smith once said the goal of production is to benefit the consumer.

And when we look at issues like the Jones Act or agribusiness subsidies or the restrictions in state law on advertising by optical firms or by pharmacies, we have to ask ourselves what is the benefit for the consumer. Perhaps the consumer will pay less for the products that are shipped between two points on the U.S. coast and there will be fewer American seamen, but the consumer saving will purchase products in the economy which will open up other jobs.

I think the problem in this country is that the trade associations are overorganized, the corporations are overorganized, the labor unions are well organized, but the consumer and the small taxpayer are not organized. I think it is the function of advocates—critics, politicians, whatever their public role may be—to do everything they can to strengthen those two constituencies into organized economic and political forces. They represent the broadest spectrum of interest in our society.

MS. SHANAHAN: What do you say, professor?

PROFESSOR HOUTHAKKER: Well, I agree with what Mr. Nader has just said. However, I would say that the actual performance leaves something to be desired, and I'm not blaming Mr. Nader or his organizations now.

I remember years ago when a question about eggs came up. There was some blatant proposal to rig the egg market, and at that time we needed some countervailing power, to quote my colleague Ken Galbraith. So I thought maybe the Consumer Federation of America, which had just been founded, would take an interest in this. But no, its leaders could not be moved, even though we provided figures proving that this would add to the price of the eggs which everybody used. They felt that the regulatory law was for the benefit of farmers, and everybody knows that farmers are poor and deserving. Somehow you never hear about the farmer who makes $100,000 a year, although there are quite a few.

In that instance, I think, the Consumer Federation of America was a little misled by the kind of thinking which you described earlier—the belief that the consumer is victimized only by large corporations. I don't think that is true. Large corporations aren't blameless, not by any means, and I'm in favor of doing various things about them, but there is a danger of seeing this too much in terms of a class struggle between the poor consumer, the poor small businessman, the poor farmer, on the one hand, and the giant corporations that oppress them, on the other. I think our reality is much more complicated than that.

Much of what happens in the area of farming, for example, isn't in the interest of farmers either. That is sometimes recognized, sometimes not.

But, as you say, we have to make it clear that the consumer is the ultimate beneficiary of our economic system. If we run it well, he benefits. If we don't, he is the one who pays. That notion, which you expressed very well, I think, is not generally accepted. There is the opposite tendency to think of the economy in more or less sociological terms, and that is one reason why deregulation has been such an uphill fight. We have had some success in the area of agriculture, for instance. We have freed up—

MR. REAGAN: Only, I think, through necessity. We finally needed everything we could produce.

PROFESSOR HOUTHAKKER: Right, but it has been an uphill fight in part because it has not always been recognized that the consumer ultimately is the one who benefits or pays.

MS. SHANAHAN: Governor, could you name two or three of your top priorities for getting rid of regulation and explain how you would go about it? In a moment I'm going to ask you what your priorities would be for keeping regulation.

MR. REAGAN: Well, I wish I had a magic answer, but the answer lies with the people of this country. And as Mr. Nader points out, the consumer is not organized. The reason probably is that it is very difficult to organize millions of consumers whose interests are so diverse. Some individual or group, for example, might want a certain product to be of better quality than it is, to reach a certain limit of quality, while other consumers might be willing to sacrifice a degree of quality in order to have the product within their price range even though it might be shoddier.

24

We have the airlines defending the fact that under the CAB they have to fly unprofitable routes in order to serve towns that do not warrant air service, while consumers who fly from here to Los Angeles and back have to pay a higher price in order to subsidize the fare on those unprofitable routes. My own belief is that if we had enough faith in the marketplace we would discover that if a town is worthy of some air attention and the major lines cannot serve it profitably, somebody will start an airline that can. The same would happen with trucks. If the big truck lines that are now routed to go through certain small towns at great expense to themselves, paid for by customers elsewhere, stopped serving the small towns, someone in those towns would say, "Hey, there is a market here for a fellow with a truck," and he'd go into business.

I challenge also the idea that most regulation is initiated by the private sector rather than by government. Now, the *Federal Register* will print 50,000 pages this year. It is one of the most remarkable printing jobs in the world—300,000 to 400,000 words every day. And if you are impatient to learn what will be in tomorrow's issue, there is a Dial-a-Register number so you can find out what regulation is going to be printed tomorrow. The *Register* averages about 25,000 new regulations a year on top of all the regulations already on the books. I don't think anyone in the private sector is asking for those.

A better explanation is that bureaucracy is so entrenched with the federal, state, and local bureaucracies that there are 15 million public employees. Each one of those must control at least another vote or vote and a half. This is a tremendous block. Congressmen have told me that they are more frightened of defying a government agency than they are of the constituency back home. These agencies have become so big and powerful that they have the capacity to destroy a congressman in his own district if they so choose. And they have the arrogance of officialdom, knowing that after the elected representatives are gone they will still be there. Their word is that we've seen you come and we'll see you go.

The only answer is for the people to be given a better

understanding of how this system of ours works, who pays for all those regulations, what those regulations mean to them and their lives. And if regulation is profiting a business, all right, let that be known, too.

But the conflicts, the duplications! Back when we were subsidizing agriculture, I uncovered an instance of six government agencies spending $35 million telling poultry raisers how to improve egg production, while a seventh government agency was spending $12 million buying surplus eggs. And this example can be matched by a thousand others.

Every program passed by Congress includes a clause that says the agency entrusted with enforcing this particular program shall make such regulations as it deems necessary, and that is the starting point. I remember hearing three congressmen trying to sell a governor's conference on the land use planning bill. We kept telling them that the so-called guidelines they were talking about would become federal mandates at the state level. Finally one congressman said more than he realized. He said: "Well, this isn't our intention at all in Congress. Of course, you realize that once we pass it, we have no control over the agency that will be enforcing it."

That's not my idea of government. I don't want to hear a congressman tell me that Congress has no control over an agency. Those fellows work for us, and they have to take the case to the people. Jefferson said, "If the people know all the facts, the people won't make a mistake." I believe the people should be protected from anything that will harm them, but I do not believe that government has a right to make decisions in our behalf. If somebody tells me that a breakfast crunchy is going to make me feel full of vitamins all day and I enjoy the taste of it, I don't want the government coming along and telling me I can't have it because it doesn't make me feel good all day. [Laughter.]

MR. NADER: Wouldn't you want the company to tell you that the so-called nutritious breakfast flake contained 40 percent sugar—before you'd even added any sugar? Your children eat those breakfast cereals.

MR. REAGAN: You are getting back into my area of protecting us from ourselves, but I—

MR. NADER: You may want to have the sugar. The purpose is to let you know that this flake is 40 percent sugar.

MR. REAGAN: Fine. I don't mind that at all, but I do question a government that can step in and tell one medium of advertising that it cannot advertise a certain product having to do with tobacco while that same government is subsidizing the growing of tobacco.

MR. NADER: I couldn't agree with you more. But I think you would also have to reflect on the fact that over the past few years very few elected officials spoke out against the self-imposed ban on advertising by lawyers, or the self-imposed ban on advertising (through state law) by pharmacies so people couldn't compare the price of pharmaceutical products. In other words, an industry will get a state law passed to prevent it from advertising so that it won't have to compete for the consumer. But let me get back to another point—

MR. REAGAN: In California, we have a law requiring stores to post the comparative prices.

MR. NADER: Finally. [Laughter.]
Let me point out one other troubling aspect of this whole regulatory situation, namely, that there is a great deal of serious violation of these regulations. Oil companies violate the Federal Energy Administration regulations. The bus companies violate the Department of Transportation safety regulations. I think it is time, if indeed we accept the rule of law, and even if we disagree with some government regulation, to call for law enforcement against corporate or business crime.

You think there is a lot of crime in the streets. There is a lot of crime in the suites, the corporate suites. It is time to enforce the law evenly, because if people feel that anyone who is powerful enough, anyone who can pay a lawyer enough, can get away with disobeying these health and safety and other regulations, respect for the law deteriorates throughout the country. Whatever our respective opinions may be on regulation, we need to pay some attention to enforcing these laws so they're not farcical, so that companies don't bribe officials here and abroad or violate environmental rules or campaign finance regulations.

PROFESSOR HOUTHAKKER: Well, one reason why there are so many violations is that there are so many laws and regulations to violate. [Laughter.]

MR. NADER: That's what the embezzler said in a New York bank: there are so many internal bank regulations that, of course, I'm going to violate some of them.

MR. REAGAN: Doesn't that bring us back to what Cicero said—that when the laws become so numerous and so complex and so confusing, society breaks down because the people can't find their way through it.

MR. NADER: All right.

MR. REAGAN: This is what I mean about losing respect for government.

MR. NADER: Some of the laws should be repealed. We need some other new laws that have long been coming. But as long as laws are on the books, you cannot tolerate flagrant, systematic, knowing violation on the grounds that these laws shouldn't, in your judgment, exist.

PROFESSOR HOUTHAKKER: You're right. I agree with that.

MR. NADER: One way to repeal the law is to enforce it.

MR. REAGAN: Yes, but wait a minute. You are using the word "law," but in this country laws are outnumbered a thousand to one by the regulations passed by bureaus to which Congress no longer pays any attention. As the congressman said, "Once we pass the bill, we don't police it any more," and the regulations take off in ways that were never intended by Congress.

MR. NADER: Until they are repealed or upset by the courts, they are still laws whether they are regulations or statutes.

MS. SHANAHAN: I'm delighted to say that our fourth panelist has arrived, Senator Hubert H. Humphrey, who is, I understand, a little frustrated because the Senate vote he was waiting for never took place. But he is ready to jump right into our discussion.

I had a question in mind when you joined us, Senator Humphrey, which is this. All of our panelists, even including Governor Reagan, seem to agree that in some areas we really do need regulation. Governor Reagan mentioned the safety of ocean liners, for example, and some of the food and health and safety requirements. But at the same time we agree that there is an unnecessarily vast amount of paperwork and in many cases too much regulation, possibly even regulations that go beyond the intent of Congress.

If you agree on these points, how, in the areas where we want to preserve regulation, do we get rid of the excesses?

HUBERT H. HUMPHREY, United States senator (Democrat, Minnesota): First, to reassess regulation you must also reassess the private market economy. Now if the private market economy is working well, if it's efficient, if there are high levels of production and price competition, you obviously don't need regulation.

However, if the market economy is not functioning well, there may be a reason for regulation. But economic regulation tends to proliferate, it tends to build. And I think for that reason it requires constant review and reassessment.

The Congress is derelict in its own responsibilities. We set up these laws, which are the incubators for regulations. The regulations are made by the people we call bureaucrats, civil servants, people who are ordinarily very well trained. You know, these bureaucrats aren't people from Mars; they are the sons and daughters of people we think of rather highly. [Laughter.] I think we ought to keep in mind that most of them are graduates of great universities —they are scientists, doctors, lawyers—experts of all sorts. But they need to have somebody taking a look to find out whether the law is being implemented or impeded or obstructed by the rules and regulations.

Now, what do we do about it? Number one, we have every committee in Congress exercise legislative oversight —which Congress has not been doing. Congress legislates, turns its programs over to the executive branch, and says, "Go to it." And they go to it; there's no doubt about that. And sometimes they go to it with a vengeance. Then you find that Congress doesn't review the rules and regulations made by the executive branch to implement the basic law it passed. Therefore, my first proposal is that every committee of Congress ought to exercise legislative oversight on every bill of any consequence, particularly those of economic or social impact.

Second, there ought to be periodic reviews of the rules and regulations from each department. Let's take, for example, the Department of Agriculture. I'm on the Committee on Agriculture and Forestry. I know a little bit about it. I have been on that committee for seventeen years. I have yet to see the secretary of agriculture volunteer information about his rules and regulations. Once in a while we ask him to come over so we can find out what he is doing, but we ought to do this on a periodic basis.

Finally, I think we need to have an economic impact study or evaluation made of every rule and regulation and every piece of legislation that we pass. For example, there now is a new Budget Committee in both the House and the Senate. Before we launch some big program, we ought to have those committees estimate the program's impact.

We did something about that today, for example, in the Defense Department's military procurement and research and development authorization bill. Too often we launch a program, and the supporters of it say, "Well, this is a little $250 million program," and, before we know it, we are down the road on a $5 billion project; and before the $5 billion project is finished, there are 2,000 people supervising it.

I say that that can be stopped. The question is, are we willing to apply ourselves to the task? We have had not only separation of powers but also separation of functions to a point where the legislative branch considers its whole role to be legislation. From there on out, the executive branch runs with it. And who are they? Well, many times they are people you have never met. [Laughter.]

I have met ambitious people in the executive branch who have an utter disdain for the legislators and who think we don't know what we are doing. Well, now, we do know what we are doing. At least if we don't, we get kicked out of office. We have no tenure; we have to face elections. Still, perhaps we could usefully combine the pragmatism of the legislator, who does compromise, with the zealousness of the civil servant or the regulator.

May I just conclude by saying some of the regulators don't do much regulating, either. Every once in a while they are captive of the very interest that they are supposed to regulate. They wear the badge that says, "I am Regulator," but it really should say, "I'm an ex-officio member of the Board of Directors of Company X"—because they really don't do much regulating.

Now, that's for openers. [Laughter.]

MS. SHANAHAN: I would like to hear what some of the other members of the panel think about your idea of more congressional oversight, including whether they feel that adds another layer of paperwork and delay and cost. Governor, aren't you surprised to find that Senator Humphrey agrees with you on so many points?

MR. REAGAN: I thought that I'd surprise him if I said thanks. He wouldn't know what I was thanking him for. [Laughter.]

SENATOR HUMPHREY: You see, governor, I still own and operate Humphrey's Drug Store. [Laughter.] And I do know something about what can happen to regulations, but that doesn't mean that I don't believe they are necessary. I am a registered pharmacist, and I know that we need regulation of drugs for the protection of the public. The FDA doesn't overregulate. It's too timid. It sometimes doesn't have enough intestines to stuff a mouse. I happen to think that it needs to do a better job of protecting people's health than it is doing. But when a man comes along from OSHA and says to you, "Look, the ceiling . . ."—

MS. SHANAHAN: Sorry—I have a no-jargon rule. OSHA is the Occupational Safety and Health Administration—right?

SENATOR HUMPHREY: That's right, but that's too long. [Laughter.]

MS. SHANAHAN: Which is enforcing, or might be failing to enforce, the relatively new law dealing with safety in places of work.

SENATOR HUMPHREY: Yes. And I think here again some basic good sense is needed. I know of an instance where an OSHA person came by and said that the ceiling was too low. What are we going to do about that? Raise the building? [Laughter.]

MR. NADER: They should have told him to crouch. [Laughter.]

SENATOR HUMPHREY: Now, there are places where the Occupational Safety—what's the rest of that?

MS. SHANAHAN: And Health Administration.

SENATOR HUMPHREY: —and Health Administration—[laughter]—is doing a very good job, and it is absolutely essential that it do it. But may I just suggest that there is no substitute for common sense.

I remember a regulator who came out to a nursing home in South Dakota where my mother was a patient. HEW had a rule that there had to be a doctor on duty all the time. Well, there was a doctor on duty, old Dr. Tschetter, who lived there in the nursing home. [Laughter.] He wasn't that old, but he had dedicated his home in memory of his beloved wife, who had died of cancer at a very young age. He had dedicated his life to it. Yet, this young fellow came in there to see me and said, "You've got to have two doctors there." I said, "Listen, buddy, my mother is in that nursing home. If I thought she needed two doctors, she would have two doctors. I'm a senator. I'm interested in what happens to Mom; but I want to tell you, Dr. Tschetter will do more work up there than any two doctors you have."

In some places nursing homes are strictly commercial. Out there, the preacher came in, the kids came in, the Ladies Aid came in, the Girl Scouts came in—they were taking care of Mom and all the other old folks there, and so was the doctor. Now, when you start applying the same rules and regulations to that nursing home and to one out here in Chevy Chase or New York, you are making a mistake. The fact that a law has been passed doesn't mean you shouldn't use your brain. [Laughter.]

MS. SHANAHAN: Yes, but how do you, in fact, legislate distinctions? Do you think it's possible to legislate a distinction between the way you regulate a nursing home in a small midwestern city and the way you regulate it in New York?

SENATOR HUMPHREY: Well, I don't know whether you can legislate the distinction, but you can have people enforce it intelligently. They can just take a look around.

For example, not long ago I was out in Morris, Minnesota—you see, I go out and look because I've got to live with my constituents—where we were taking the mentally retarded out of those big institutions where they are treated more like cattle than like people and were putting them into group homes. We have a man and wife who care for six or seven of these retarded people like a family. Now, HEW has rules that say you've got to have so many square feet per person in this sort of home. I know that's important. It just so happens that this particular home was short one square foot. [Laughter.] Now that's a fact.

[Laughter.] So HEW sent one person back to an institution. That person was destroyed. That person had been coming out of his shell, out of the misery of the big institution, and had been blossoming. He was a little boy, fourteen years old, and his life was crushed. Not only that, but it turned out that no one had measured the closet space in this boy's room, and that there was actually enough space. Now, I did something about it—I just raised hell, to put it bluntly. [Laughter.]

That's what senators have to do, but I shouldn't have to spend my time on that. All that particular situation took was somebody with enough brains to say simply, "This is a minor violation. These people look happy. They are well fed. They are well cared for." The lady of the house said, "You know, senator, they asked me all about the square footage, they asked me all about the electrical outlets, they asked me all about the beds, but nobody asked me if I loved these people." I want to tell you, I know a little bit about mental retardation. My wife and I have spent a lot of time on this subject. When I find a regulator who doesn't have enough sense to ask the right question or enough sense to realize that somebody really cares about the patients, then I know what needs to be done about reforming regulation. Now, that's why I say there can be some variables.

MR. NADER: Government agencies so often dwell on trivia and forget the more important purposes of their operation. For example, the job safety agency we were just talking about has avoided facing up to setting standards for major chemicals that thousands and thousands of workers are exposed to and that are harmful; and yet it will often zero in on some trivial violation. And, of course, people who oppose job safety laws pick on these trivial things to try to discredit the laws themselves. The Federal Trade Commission used to do that years ago. It filed a case against collusive marketing of bull semen and forgot about the Generals—General Electric, General Motors, General Mills, General Foods—and Colonel Sanders. [Laughter.] This is what discredits a lot of regulation.

SENATOR HUMPHREY: Yes.

MR. NADER: At the national level the regulators work on small businesses that can't fight back as readily and forget about the big issues and the big abuses. But I agree, getting back to congressional oversight—there's more of it now than there used to be—

SENATOR HUMPHREY: Yes, by far.

MR. NADER: —but it needs to be developed in two important directions. First, agencies should be expected to report on how their laws are being enforced or violated. You really learn a lot about an agency's impact, in all areas, from compliance reports.

The second function of the Congress should be to establish a Civil Service accountability law, so that if people around the country are abused by a civil servant they have got a handle. They can challenge and petition for the person to be disciplined or for a review of the government decision. Right now, the only people who really can do that are people who are very well heeled, with very powerful lawyers in Washington—

SENATOR HUMPHREY: Or they come to their congressmen.

MR. NADER: —or they come to their congressmen.

SENATOR HUMPHREY: We spend 60 percent of our time on casework. A lot of people don't agree with my point of view, but my constituents know that if they come to me with a problem, I'm going to rip up the turf until we get an answer. And that's what you have to do around here. Love doesn't work in this city very much, I regret to say. [Laughter.] You really have to be a—Ralph, you know what I mean—you've got to kind of go at them. [Laughter.]

MR. REAGAN: Senator, I think your question gets down to the root of the problem with most of the regulations— namely, how do we make these exceptions you're talking about? You and I could sit here and exchange stories about this type of bureaucratic know-nothingness and failure of common sense. But isn't the answer really that we have tried to centralize too much government at the national level; that you can't make a myriad of rules that will fit every corner of this country, across 3,000 miles; that we need more government control and management, particularly of these human problems, back at the local level?

SENATOR HUMPHREY: Governor, I don't disagree with that at all. All I ask is that local government be willing to pay the freight to get competence.

I have been a mayor of a city and I have spent a good deal of time working with state and local government officials and legislators. Regrettably, in many of the cities and counties—and particularly at the county level in rural areas—the health departments are not adequate. The engineering departments are not adequate. They cut corners. I hate to say that, but it's a fact. Now, with revenue sharing and so on, maybe we can help them firm up.

I do agree that if we are going to have flexibility, we've got to have the people living close to the problem enforcing the rules, and more and more authority has to be vested at the local level. But, believe me, the standards of government in some counties make you wonder whether the local authority is really going to protect the public interest.

MR. REAGAN: Yes, but senator—and you and I know we won't be on the same side on this—I think that this is partly because the federal government has usurped the revenue that ought to remain in the place where it was raised, at the state and local level on down. You see, revenue sharing would not be necessary if we left the revenue at the local level and restricted the federal government to those tasks which properly belong to it, the area of national defense and so forth. Let the federal government set the minimum standards which must be met. To me revenue sharing means that the money is collected and passed through those puzzle palaces on the Potomac, and then it comes back to us minus a carrying charge. [Laughter.]

SENATOR HUMPHREY: But at least you get the money. Let me say, governor, in my state, for example, we have a state income tax.

MR. REAGAN: So do we.

SENATOR HUMPHREY: We have a good one. But I know two or three states right up here along the eastern seaboard that don't.

MS. SHANAHAN: New Jersey, New Hampshire—

SENATOR HUMPHREY: We didn't usurp their revenue. They can institute a state income tax. The money is there. The only reason the federal government uses this taxing power is that it alone is able to tax a large interstate corporation, for example, to tap the sources of revenue that are out there.

MR. REAGAN: But on that subject of taxing business— and before you came, business took some abuse up here that it didn't deserve, along with some that it did—isn't it true that when we tax business to remove some of the burden from the so-called little man, the little man winds up paying, because a business tax has to be incorporated in the price of the product—

MS. SHANAHAN: I think I'm going to let you end on that—

SENATOR HUMPHREY: Oh, wait a minute. Don't let us end yet. We're just getting going. [Laughter.]

MR. REAGAN: Only people pay taxes.

SENATOR HUMPHREY: Only people pay taxes, but there is some equity and some equality of performance when taxes are paid. Not everybody can spend two weeks in the Caribbean on a yacht, but I'll guarantee you that you can spend a week on Lake Calhoun, in Minneapolis, if you want to, or you can spend some time in one of our public parks. In my opinion, many of the services that are provided out of tax funds—good roads, good schools, good public health offices, good parks and recreational facilities —are fringe benefits that go to a citizen that he would never get otherwise, unless he were well-to-do.

MS. SHANAHAN: There's no fair place to stop this exchange, so I'm going to have to be arbitrary—stop. [Laughter and applause.] We've been straying a little from the subject of regulation and deregulation, but now we can get back to the heart of the matter with questions from the audience.

BARBARA FRANKLIN, commissioner, Consumer Product Safety Commission: I am a regulator, and as such have been fascinated by this discussion. A number of the panelists have touched on my concern, so I would like to direct my question to all of you.

My question has to do with the accountability of someone like me, a regulator who is making regulatory decisions for the public and in the interest of the public. My agency has the mission of protecting the public against unreasonable risks of injury associated with everyday consumer products used at home and in recreation. Now, first, in making decisions to that effect, I want to know as much as I can. I want to know what the consumer's side is, what the impact on business is, and whether the proposed action really is in the public interest.

Second, I am not elected. I am a person appointed by the President, confirmed by the Senate, for a fixed term, seven years. I'm going to make a lot of decisions in seven years—decisions that are going to affect a lot of people's lives and commit a lot of dollars. How do I know that what I'm doing is what the public wants me to do?

I am concerned about that, because I could be very insulated. I don't see enough institutionalized mechanisms to make sure that I do my job in the public interest. I'm concerned from my own standpoint and from the standpoint of my agency, too. I think there need to be more guarantees but I would like to hear your thoughts on what can be done to ensure that a variety of government officials like me are really doing what the public wants done.

MR. HUMPHREY: In the first place, the representatives of the public are elected. We have accountability: the House of Representatives confronts it every two years; the Senate, every six years.

We have another kind of accountability. I go home practically every weekend and I have eight to ten to twelve meetings during my so-called recess at which I stand before an audience to be asked questions, or open up an office, or sit in the county courthouse and listen to the people who come through. I'm held accountable for your regulations. Therefore, I think it is necessary for me as a member of Congress to have an opportunity in the Congress to review with you once in a while what I hear about how those regulations are affecting people's lives.

I also get an awful lot of mail. One of the things that I regret about the Civil Service is that bureaucrats don't have the sensitivity to mail that we have as members of Congress. If they did, I wouldn't have to handle hundreds of Social Security cases every month that ultimately are resolved simply because the word "senator" has been attached. If a complaint were in the name of my sister or somebody else it wouldn't get any place. It would just go through the mails and get filed away and be given some routine answer. But the minute the name of a congressman is added to a request, they blue-strip it or blue-label it or red-label it and, bingo, something happens. That means that something *can* happen, but it ought to happen without a congressman picking up the telephone and asking, "Say, what have you done here?"

I think Congress and the regulatory agencies ought to have a cooperative relationship, because those of us in Congress who passed that law instructed you to write the rules and regulations. That makes us accomplices to either the good deed or the crime.

MS. SHANAHAN: Would anyone else like to answer that question?

MR. REAGAN: Yes. I find myself wondering how many hundreds of people must never have thought to write to their congressman or take their case to the governor or the state legislator. But isn't it possible to do some reviews within an agency? Suppose a regulation comes down concerning some particular household implement and you suddenly find yourself required to upset a lot of households, to say nothing of a lot of merchants, in order to enforce it. At a time like that can't an agency call for a review and say, "Wait a minute. What has been the record? Has this particular thing caused any problems up until now?"

As we were saying earlier, although Mr. Nader thought maybe we were dwelling on outstanding cases, it is true that there are many instances, particularly in the safety field, in which the regulation was created because someone talked to someone or heard something and then presented what sounded like a good idea to well-meaning people like yourself; but when the records were checked it was discovered that not a single problem had ever arisen from this particular instrument or implement. In that instance it would seem to me that the agency itself, someone in the agency, should have a cabinet meeting and say, "Hey, what are we doing with this rule? No one has ever been burned by this or hurt by this or pinched by this," or whatever it might be.

I have already cited the example of a toy. There was also a case recently involving a solvent for cleaning windshields. Suddenly, the government picked up 2,495 cans of this solvent because the label did not say "Cannot be made non-poisonous" and because the cap was not childproof. But they didn't send them back to the manufacturer to have the labels changed and the caps put on. The agency simply confiscated and destroyed them.

Again, it is a matter of that common sense you were talking about. But at the agency level, can't common sense be applied to the overall purpose? Can't you ask of a regulation, "Are we trying to cure an ill that doesn't exist?"

MS. SHANAHAN: I think Barbara Franklin's question, though, was really, how does she find out what the public thinks is common sense?

COMMISSIONER FRANKLIN: That's right. Through what mechanisms can I find out, on a day-to-day basis or on any kind of systematic basis, what the public wants? That worries me.

MR. NADER: Let me make a few suggestions based on long experience, some of it bitter. One, you need input in the form of information from hearings, letters, and inventors, processed in a meaningful way. All of this is pouring into the agency but it is not given a systematic and organized meaning.

You need participation by consumers, the people who are to ultimately benefit by your efforts. That means you need the kind of regulatory reform that gives consumers the rights, the remedies, and the representation to participate in proposing that a new safety standard, for example, be issued or that one be revoked or refined. I know that your agency opens its files and its meetings probably more ambitiously than many other government agencies, but no consumer groups have adequate staffs or resources to make use of so much information.

You also need to be afraid that you are going to lose your job before your term is up. It is an axiom in Washington, I think, that one of the best ways to lose your job is to do your job. The people who blow the whistle on corruption or waste, as Ernie Fitzgerald did in the Department of Defense, lose their jobs.

I think that if the public is given rights so that if, say, you refused to enforce the law and they were harmed, if an injurious product were improperly allowed on the market, the public should have some sort of feedback that allows it to question your fitness to remain in office. Now, that sort of feedback and input will make you much more accountable, I think; but more important, it will give you strength and support so you can stand up against the more organized special interests that distort and often manipulate an agency's operations.

I might say, Governor Reagan, that the Consumer Product Safety Commission disputes your interpretation of those 2,000 cans of windshield cleaner. The commission simply said that if the problem could not be corrected, the cans could not be sold. The company decided not to correct it, so they were destroyed.

MR. REAGAN: Well, I don't know. That isn't the way it was reported to me. It was reported that the company never had a chance to correct the cans; they were simply confiscated and destroyed.

SENATOR HUMPHREY: I think one thing you have to keep in mind in all of this is that a certain number of people are never going to want to be regulated at all. Some time ago Congress passed what we call the Prescription Drug Act, which made certain types of drugs available only by prescription—because a lot of sleeping pills, barbiturates, and so on simply had to be regulated. But we got a lot of heat from that. A lot of people want to be able to go in and buy these drugs off the rack, as if they were peppermint lifesavers.

You would be surprised at the amount of heat that you get when you start putting regulations on some things, and it costs a little extra. But I'll tell you what happens. If, for example, a regulation on an electrical appliance isn't adequate to be protective and a person gets a shock or a serious injury, then that's much more serious than somebody writing a letter to say that he or she didn't like the regulation that you had on it. It's difficult to strike a balance. I guess all I'm trying to say is this: if you are in public life and think people are going to like you for what you do, you are in the wrong business. You ought to run one of those ice cream wagons—what was it? Good Humor wagon. [Laughter.]

MS. SHANAHAN: And then the mothers won't like you, because their children are getting tooth decay. [Laughter.]
I think we had better go to our next question.

COMMISSIONER FRANKLIN: You are touching on a very

crucial point there, senator. It's the problem of having to balance the benefits of a regulation—how many lives are we going to save, how many injuries are we going to eliminate—against the cost—who is going to pay and is that too much. These are hard decisions. My concern is that over a period of time I get enough systematic feedback, either from the Congress—you people who are elected—or from whatever segments of the population are affected, so I know that what I'm doing is really what the public thinks is the right thing to do.

SENATOR HUMPHREY: And you want to be sure you are hearing the public, and not just some of the public.

COMMISSIONER FRANKLIN: Yes, that's right.

SENATOR HUMPHREY: Because some very, very loud noises can come from a very small group that represents a grandmother and an ex-mother-in-law, and that's about it. Much of the mail that we get in Congress comes from very intense little groups preoccupied with some little issue about which the average member of the public is not concerned. But all at once, you are persuaded that this issue is a major problem. You go on home and run around the country looking for these people, and they are hard to find.

WESLEY J. LIEBELER, Office of Policy Planning, Federal Trade Commission and UCLA Law School: In listening to the conversation that just occurred, and particularly to Senator Humphrey's remark, I was struck that you wanted to make sure that you heard all of the people, not just some of them. I suggest that there is one indicator that is sensitive to all of the people most of the time, and that is the marketplace. Which, of course, suggests that perhaps we ought not to have quite as much government regulation as we have, in order to place a greater degree of reliance on the market forces.

That leads me to the question I wanted to ask Mr. Nader. He asked Governor Reagan to provide a list of the subsidies to business that the governor would get rid of;

and then, in response to the governor's point that the proliferation of laws and regulations in this country, particularly at the federal level, has led to disrespect if not contempt for the law, Mr. Nader said that many of these laws and regulations should be repealed. Now, I assume, from what Mr. Nader has said in the past, that he would agree that perhaps the Civil Aeronautics Board and the Interstate Commerce Commission should be abolished, for starters. But I would like Mr. Nader to give us a list of other government agencies and other government regulations that he would get rid of, and why.

MR. NADER: Do you want it now? [Laughter.]

MR. LIEBELER: Yes sir.

MR. NADER: The Maritime Administration, a good deal of the Department of Commerce, a good deal of the Department of Interior, a good deal of the Department of Defense, portions of the GSA—I mean, we can go on forever. I could even suggest some in your agency.

MR. LIEBELER: Which ones, and why?

MR. NADER: The textile, furs, and wool labeling operations—which are a waste of time, because they're not being done right and because it would work best to abolish them and incorporate them into other functions of the commission.

MS. SHANAHAN: Wait a minute. Ralph Nader, are you for taking out that tag that tells me whether I can wash my blouse in the washing machine?

MR. NADER: No, indeed. It is a question about the bureaucracy that I am raising. We are spending too much money to perform simple tasks. We don't need a vested interest with excessive employee levels to perform that job. Now, a lot of times—

MS. SHANAHAN: You didn't answer my question.

MR. NADER: No—I'm for it. That's the care labeling rule you're referring to. I'm for it. What I am advocating is a new way of abolishing government waste. The function may be important, but it has become overorganized and overstaffed.

The problem is that some sections of the FTC have always been very close to industry; they arbitrate various squabbles and waste a lot of money. And they don't really use their resources to represent the consumer, as they should. I'm not just saying some of the agency's functions are worthless, so therefore abolish the agency. I'm saying some of the agency's functions are valued, but it does not need the kind of staff and the bureaucracy it now has to perform them. I think Bob Townsend, who wrote the book *Up The Organization* once suggested that the Department of Agriculture strip itself down to 10 percent of its staff and predicted that productivity would go up. That is the kind of experiments we should try.

SENATOR HUMPHREY: If the Department of Agriculture had had a few more inspectors in its Grain Inspection Division there wouldn't be a national scandal over grain inspection right now.

MR. NADER: Or a few honest inspectors, who were on the job. [Laughter.]

SENATOR HUMPHREY: Well, no. The point is that the inspectors who were causing the trouble were private, licensed inspectors. The Department of Agriculture inspectors did their job and did it well.

MR. NADER: But they knew about it—

SENATOR HUMPHREY: It was the private licensing feature, which was a conflict of interest, that caused much of this trouble.

Let me say a word about CAB. I come from a state that has got little towns. We know that in order to have industry in our little towns—take a town like Worthington, Minnesota—we have to wage big battles with the CAB. It's really unethical for a senator to appear before the CAB on behalf of one of his constituents, but that didn't bother me one bit. [Laughter.] I went right up there and said, "I want North Central Airlines to come into Worthington, Minnesota." Now, if we had left that to the marketplace, they would have bypassed Worthington. As a matter of fact, the railroads would bypass practically every little farm town we have. They want to run between the big terminals. And the trucks would bypass them all, too. Now, if you feel that smaller towns—towns of 1,000 or 2,000 people or even 600 or 700 people—shouldn't have a truck or a railroad, if you feel that a town of 5,000 shouldn't have an airline coming into it, all you have to do is abolish the CAB and all the regulations in transportation. And those towns will dry up faster than a pot of water on the Sahara Desert in a blazing sun.

One has to balance the advantages and disadvantages of CAB regulation because, of course, those major airlines don't make any money by going into small towns. To go to the small towns is to provide a service. It's like rural free mail delivery. There are a lot of city-slickers who don't think farmers ought to get their mail, either.

Frankly, the farmers ought to have a computer service that gets market prices out to them so they can stay in the marketplace and not be swindled by grain trade speculators. That is really needed in this country. Maybe one of these days we will start to send printouts right into the homes of the American people, instead of delayed daily newspapers, so that they will know what the market conditions are. In this fast-moving economy, that is what is needed.

Now, what's the answer? Do you think a town of 5,000 or 10,000 people that wants to have a little industry that is part of a major industry, let us say, with its central office in Chicago, should be denied that opportunity because the executives say, "If we can't fly into your airport, we are not going to come into your town"? Do you think our towns ought to dry up?

MR. LIEBELER: Senator, I'm not one of those city-slickers. I was born in a town in North Dakota of 1,200 people and

I graduated from Macalester College, where you once were a professor of political science.

SENATOR HUMPHREY: Well, then, you understand my problem.

MR. LIEBELER: Yes. And I just want to ask you, who is going to pay for the service that the people in these small towns get?

SENATOR HUMPHREY: The people.

MR. LIEBELER: Who? Not the people in Worthington, Minnesota. The market would provide that service if—

SENATOR HUMPHREY: Well, may I ask who is paying for New York? Who is paying for a lot of us?

MR. LIEBELER: Well, I am. [Laughter.]

SENATOR HUMPHREY: We all pay for each other. Do we want a country or don't we? Do we want a society in which people have a chance to grow and to develop? It costs more money to give people a good education in communities that don't have good tax bases. In my state we have equality of educational opportunity. We tax people in Edina, Minnesota, which is a rich suburb of Minneapolis, in order to provide a good education in Cook, Minnesota or in Floodwood, Minnesota, and we consider that good social practice. And we make no apologies, sir—Macalester College or not. [Laughter.] A lot of people who went to Macalester College got a lot of help from other people, too. When I taught there I helped raise money from some of the rich people around in order to give others educational opportunities. I don't know when you went there, but I taught there the two years that I lost out; you remember that? [Laughter and applause.]

How about the Rural Electrification Administration? Don't you believe farmers ought to have electricity? If you didn't have electricity for farmers, buddy, you'd be starving. [Laughter.]

MR. REAGAN: Senator, we part company here because that line of thought would mean that Salinas, California and St. Louis, Missouri and Mankato, Minnesota and a few other towns would be taxed to bail New York City out for being the most mismanaged city in the United States. Earlier I made the point that if the CAB were done away with and smaller towns lost some of their mainline service, the marketplace would find that there was business for a certain type of airline into those communities and would provide it.

SENATOR HUMPHREY: Governor, you're blowing bubbles. [Laughter.]

MR. REAGAN: No, I'm not, senator.

SENATOR HUMPHREY: Let me tell you what the railroads do. Every time they feel they can't make a dollar, they abandon trackage. Abandon enough trackage, and you won't get groceries. [Laughter.]

MR. REAGAN: I don't think so. I think that part of the small communities' troubles would be solved by someone who would find it profitable, with a truck or whatever, to bring these supplies in. I claim that in recent years, mainly the last four decades, we have not tried the magic of the marketplace.

Mr. Nader responded to the challenge from his questioner by naming some of the agencies that he was really going to eliminate, and I thought for a minute there he and I had become blood brothers. [Laughter.] I have a proposal as to how we might find out what we could eliminate. After eight years in public office, I have a sneaking suspicion that if all of us in government just quietly sneaked home some day and shut the door, it would be weeks before the people ever missed us. [Laughter and applause.]

SENATOR HUMPHREY: Governor, that's exactly the way I felt those two years I was out of office. [Laughter.]

MR. REAGAN: We could stay away until we found out what it was the people missed, and then restore that.

But I would like to ask about the education situation in Minnesota. We've had this problem in California, also. I believe in a minimum standard. I believe in state support to local education that still allows local control but sets a floor.

SENATOR HUMPHREY: Yes, sir.

MR. REAGAN: But there are a great many areas—I don't know whether Minnesota is one—where that philosophy has been carried to the point where a ceiling has also been set and a local district that wants to tax itself more to provide better education is told it can't do that because everybody can't do it.

SENATOR HUMPHREY: Well, we went to school; we are not that stupid, governor. We provide a basic floor—and it's a high floor. It's called, if I may say, the Minnesota Miracle in Education. [Laughter.] It is so described, and I'm very proud of it.

We talk about everybody's having to pay his own way, but how would you like to be living out in Nevada, for example, if you couldn't have a federal highway system going through there? How are you going to develop the remote parts of the country? The postal system, the highway system, the transportation system, the rural electric system, the irrigation systems—look, they tax us in Minnesota for irrigation projects out in the West. Why, that beautiful valley you have out there in California, governor, gets a lot of water. If you don't believe it, ask the folks in Arizona who think you get too much. [Laughter.] And a lot of that water comes out of federal appropriations for irrigation projects. I vote for those programs because I believe this is one country. I was brought up to believe that this is the United States of America. I believe that people may move from Worthington, Minnesota to San Francisco, or from New York out into a small town like Mankato, Minnesota and expect to find that there are basic minimum standards in this country for every human being.

MR. REAGAN: I agree.

MS. SHANAHAN: Let's go on to the next question.

MERRILL BROWN, Media General Services: We seem to have been avoiding a subject that is very popular in Washington now, and that is the Ford administration's initiatives in this area. I am interested in knowing what the panelists, particularly those who have expressed presidential aspirations, at least in the past, think about the Ford initiatives in regulatory reform.

SENATOR HUMPHREY: I've been trying to work on the President's last regulatory reform, decontrolling oil, and I haven't had much time to take a look at that other little document that came up here, because we have been trying to do something to help the American consumer on the question of energy. So, quite honestly, I haven't had a chance to study the President's proposal. It may be a very, very good one.

But I did hear the President talking the other day about how bad some of the regulatory commissions were, and I can give him one suggestion right here tonight. I was vice-president of the United States. Vice-presidents generally don't have enough to do, and they sometimes get into trouble because they don't. I suggest that the President appoint his vice-president to chair a national commission to take a look at all these regulatory devices, agencies, techniques and rules, and to report back to the President and the Congress within a year. That would give the vice-president a full-scale job and would help a lot more than just giving speeches to the effect that all regulation of business is bad.

May I suggest too that the President of the United States has a lot of authority over many of these bad regulations. He has authority over the Department of Interior, over all the executive departments, although not over the quasi-public independent agencies like the FPC, for those are congressional bodies. But he has a lot of authority.

If the President wants to send us a proposal, fine and good. I hope that we will look at it in a constructive manner. I don't prejudge it. But I know that if the President of the United States thinks there are too many regulations in the Department of Agriculture, he can call Secretary Earl Butz over and say, "Hey, Earl, let's do something about it." And if he thinks there is too much regulation in the Department of Commerce, he can do something about that, too, because he has the power to appoint a secretary and an undersecretary. He has great power—and let's quit playing games with it. You know he's got it and I know he's got it. If he wants to use his vice-president, he can set up a commission—we've had commissions for everything in this country—and we can take a look at what the regulations are. And he can put Governor Reagan on the commission right off the bat, give him a full-time job. [Laughter.]

MR. REAGAN: I volunteer. Have axe, will travel. [Laughter.]

SENATOR HUMPHREY: That's sharp. [Laughter.]

MS. SHANAHAN: Do we have a question over here?

RITA RICARDO CAMPBELL, Hoover Institution on War, Revolution and Peace: Among other things, I'm a member of the National Advisory Drug Committee. At the first meeting of the committee I attended, I was amazed to find a letter presented to the members of the committee, signed by twenty physicians, mostly academics involved in research (I remember Dr. De Bakey's name) from about every major medical school in the country, saying that there was a lag in approval of prescription drugs in the United States, as compared with other countries, specifically Great Britain.

At the beginning of this Round Table, one of the panelists stated that you could not prove that people had died because a drug was not approved in the United States, although it had been abroad. Rifampin, which cures tuberculosis, was approved in Italy in 1968, but it was not approved in the United States until many years later. Every year that passed during that period, there were 3,500 to 5,000 deaths in the United States, because the drug was not available. I could cite a long list of drugs with similar

51

histories, but rather than do that I suggest that people check the medical literature, specifically the writings of William Wardell, who is both an M.D. and a Ph.D. at the University of Rochester.

My question, addressed to Ralph Nader, is on what basis did he say we could not prove that there was a drug lag when Commissioner Schmidt in recent testimony admitted there was a drug lag in the United States, and that it has now been corrected in many areas.

MR. NADER: If you studied the regulation of drugs around the world, you would see that many countries rely on the Food and Drug Administration's tests and results and findings for their own work. We do the work for a lot of countries abroad.

Second, there is a drug lag in another sense, in the removal of worthless or dangerous drugs from the marketplace under the 1962 drug amendments. Panalba, for example, which was killing and injuring thousands of people every year, according to the Academy of Science's report on it, was on the market for a number of years because of that kind of drug lag.

Third, it is very easy to say "x" drug in Italy cures tuberculosis, without also going into its side effects and the availability of other drugs, already approved, that can deal with a similar medical problem.

We can't debate every point in great detail here, but I'd like to offer those three factors as a framework for analysis. Anybody who wants to pursue this matter further can contact our Health Research Group and study the evidence that it has obtained from around the world in the medical literature.

DR. CAMPBELL: I agree that this is a very difficult subject for people who are mere consumers. I am not a physician. And even the physicians do not agree. The conclusions of the double blind clinical studies, done by one group of physicians in one particular hospital, differ from those of another group of physicians who performed exactly the same tests on a drug. There is agreement, however, that the United States did lag. The economic literature shows it. I think we would agree that this is a difficult subject for consumers to understand, but we are in a very mobile society and it is important for the people in the United States to learn more about it, for their own sakes.

SENATOR HUMPHREY: Could I just add that the testing procedures are much more strict and prolonged in the United States than they are in other countries.

DR. CAMPBELL: And that is causing our researchers to go abroad.

SENATOR HUMPHREY: Well, no. Many of these new drugs are very powerful, and while they do have curative effects, they also have, as Ralph Nader has said, serious side effects. We have known that; and that is why we have had to be very careful. A number of drugs have been taken off the market. Recently, a diabetic drug was taken off the market because it had very serious side effects. I tell you, we have to be exceedingly careful.

People's body chemistries vary widely and sometimes a drug reacts on one person differently than it does on another. Anybody who has ever had any problem with cancer knows this. I lost a brother. Before he died, I want to tell you, I was desperate to get any kind of a drug I had ever heard about. There was always somebody coming up with some new drug that was going to make the miracle cure. For one person there is a cure, for another, just a remission. People are very, very different in their cellular structure, and it's just essential that we be very, very careful. Antibiotic drugs are very dangerous yet very powerful drugs. How would you like to be the responsible person at the FDA when you've got, let's say, five different conclusions on a drug and its effects from ten different hospitals? What is your duty then? Your duty is to be hesitant and at least protective of the public health and the individual. We are suing doctors all over the country for malpractice, not only because of surgery, but also because of prescriptions.

MR. REAGAN: Senator, I know that England is now ahead of us in the production of health-giving drugs, and England's policy has been, I think, reasonably careful. It is not to ban a drug because of the potential ill effect on some small percentage of individuals, because of the possibility of an allergic reaction to it. I have been told by doctors that under the present FDA rules, penicillin could not be licensed because there are people who are severely allergic to penicillin. But isn't it possible that if we find that there is this possibility of side effects but also that a drug has great curative power for a great number of people, it could be marketed with safeguards and warnings to the medical profession about the tests that must be made on an individual before it can be safely applied.

SENATOR HUMPHREY: That is regularly done, governor. In fact, the FDA has gone to great lengths to require the proper information in every packet of drugs for doctors.

MR. REAGAN: But, now, in England, they follow this drug through the regular marketplace and accumulate records on years of experience with its use. So it isn't a matter of America accepting the opinion of a foreign medical service that, perhaps, isn't up to our standard; it is a matter of looking at their record—let's say they have used the drug for five years, that so many hundred thousand people have used it, and that here are the results—and concluding that that's enough for us. Americans aren't that different from—

SENATOR HUMPHREY: May I say, governor, we try these drugs frequently in what we call public hospitals—general hospitals, veterans' hospitals, hospitals that receive public funds—and the first time somebody is a victim of a bad side effect of a drug, there is a national scandal. Those are the hospitals where new drugs are tried. You've got to get consent—

MR. REAGAN: Well, I don't think drugs should be tried there any more than any place else.

SENATOR HUMPHREY: Well, you don't just market a drug and say, "Hey, everybody, take a look at it, and see what happens."

MR. REAGAN: No. No one is advocating that.

SENATOR HUMPHREY: You've got to have testing systems, and you can't test these drugs in a laboratory; you have to test them on individuals. And that is why the testing process has to be selective and why it has to be very carefully worked out. In fact, we have raised Cain with the FDA in the past because its testing process was not good enough. Do you remember the drug Thalidomide?

MR. REAGAN: We discussed that earlier, before you came.

SENATOR HUMPHREY: And there are many other drugs that have had very serious side effects, producing blindness and other serious problems.

MR. NADER: Birth control pills—for example, in England they were much more careful about the marketing of birth control pills than we were in the United States, which shows that the roles are sometimes reversed. And now, after a number of years, discussions are appearing in the medical literature about the increasing mortality levels attributed to birth control pills, particularly high potency birth control pills. So we've got to be extremely careful, not only for the well-being of individuals, but for their progeny's well-being, when these powerful drugs are put on the market.

Also there are just dozens and dozens of drugs that were deemed dangerous and/or ineffective by the National Academy of Sciences panels pursuant to the 1962 drug amendments which were not taken off the market until many years later. Some of them are still on the market now, including billions of dollars worth of worthless over-the-counter drugs.

MS. SHANAHAN: Let's go on to the next question.

STEVE MOTT, *Washington Post*: Governor Reagan, as I interpret your remarks, you are opposed to any regulation that would keep fares or prices from decreasing—for example, regulation by the ICC or the CAB. Now, what do you do when a large company that has great financial resources engages in predatory pricing, for the purpose of driving smaller, less financially able companies out of business and creating a monopoly situation?

MR. REAGAN: I think this is what we have a Federal Trade Commission for—and I am not opposed to anything that would keep prices from going down. As a matter of fact, I would like to hear what the gentlemen on this panel would say to a suggestion that we pass a statute or a constitutional amendment to the effect that the government can't stop a company from lowering a price. But I also know that the Federal Trade Commission's lot has been distorted in recent years. The federal trade laws have created situations where major corporations, once they have produced a product that in open competition captures a great deal of the market because it happens to be just what the public wanted, are fearful of lowering the price. If they marketed the product at the price they could actually provide it for, they would capture even more of the market—and they would be in trouble.

Now, I know this from personal experience with one of the Generals, General Electric. At one stage, some years ago, GE could produce light bulbs for half the price at which it was selling them and was in open competition with Sylvania and Westinghouse and all the others. But GE already had such a large share of the market that it didn't dare reduce the price as low as it could have, because if it had captured any more of the market, it would have been in trouble with the government.

There again we come up against the conflicts that occur between bureaus and agencies. A gentleman who was for a long time in the Federal Trade Commission has written a book about situations where companies found themselves charged, under legislation that is on the books, both with price fixing at a lower price, and with not making a differential in their price in different markets. And

56

there was no way that companies could be guilty simultaneously of both.

A few years ago General Motors produced a Chevrolet model that captured so much of the small car market that the Chevrolet division was openly hoping and praying that Ford would come up with something exciting, because GM was afraid of what would happen if it captured any more of that particular market. As for the big merchant who sells at prices below cost and absorbs his loss in order to drive the other fellow out of business, I think that with the FTC and fair trade laws, this can be adequately controlled.

MS. SHANAHAN: Professor Houthakker, I know that this question is right up your alley of expertise and I would like to hear what you have to say.

PROFESSOR HOUTHAKKER: Well, I would say that one purpose of reducing ICC regulation or CAB regulation is to leave more scope for antitrust laws where they are applicable. Predatory pricing by a transportation company, if it were no longer illegal under ICC regulations, would still be illegal under antitrust laws.

Of course, when it comes to the problem of market shares that Governor Reagan mentioned, I think, as a believer in competition, that in some cases divestiture—breaking up large corporations—may be the only solution. I, too, deplore the situation where a company feels that it cannot expand because if it did it would drive out competitors who are not viable.

MS. SHANAHAN: Is the only solution to Chevrolet's dilemma, which Governor Reagan described, to make a separate auto company out of the Chevrolet division of GM?

PROFESSOR HOUTHAKKER: A definite answer would have to depend on a detailed study of the production structure of the automobile industry. I would certainly not rule out your suggestion. I think that there are situations where something like that may be necessary. After all, we accept the fact that individuals die and leave their property to heirs. Corporations, I think, should not be regarded as necessarily immortal. There has to be a certain generational turnover in corporations, as well as in individuals, up to a point.

MARJORIE MILLER, *Ramparts* magazine and National Citizens' Committee for Broadcasting: I would like to get back to the food industry and ex-Governor Reagan's breakfast habits. I understand that it is your right to eat sweet, crunchy cereal if you want to, but isn't it also your right to know that you are paying fifty-two cents a box for this cereal, which contains a half-cent worth of vitamins, because corporate farmers control the food industry? And if you think that it is your right to know, how do you propose that the consumer find this out, when the same corporate control encompasses the media?

MR. REAGAN: I can't go along with the premise that corporate farmers control the food industry, because corporate farming provides only about 2 percent of the agricultural production of America; and even some of that 2 percent is made up of family corporations that have been incorporated for various tax purposes.

SENATOR HUMPHREY: We agree.

MR. REAGAN: All right. [Laughter.]

MS. MILLER: I would like to hear Mr. Nader's comments on this. And I would like to suggest that you read *Eat Your Heart Out,* by Jim Hightower.

MR. NADER: The point of the question is well taken, even though the questioner focused on corporate farmers. She should have mentioned the whole processing industry.

The fact is that cereal now costs about $1.20 a pound. And what are you getting in terms of nutrition? Enormous amounts of sugar that are filling our children's bodies and will have debilitating effects later. Is the consumer entitled to know where the markups come from—the middle man, packaging, advertisement and other factors? Is it profit or does it result from inefficiencies? Is the consumer entitled to compare the levels of nutrition of different breakfast cereals so that he can choose, not on the basis of what little plastic doo-dad is in the box or whether there is a big rooster on the cover, but whether it's really meritorious food?

MR. REAGAN: Well, sometimes I like to eat something just because it tastes good. [Applause.]

MR. NADER: That's true. That's what dessert is for, governor. [Laughter.]

MR. REAGAN: My mother always told me carrots tasted good. [Laughter.]

SENATOR HUMPHREY: I'm not too far from you, governor, on this. I realize that people have a right to make some choices. I don't think we just want to prescribe diets. We do need some nutrition education in the country.

MR. REAGAN: Yes.

SENATOR HUMPHREY: And we need a good deal of it. And I think it's good to have labeling on a food package so people can find out what is in it. A lot of people don't read labels, but they ought to have that right.

Finally, I would simply say that a lot of the cost in everything we do today lies in the whole process of merchandising, processing, and growth; and everybody gets a little piece of the action. That is why people have jobs. You know, it's just like this business of the price of a loaf of bread. Even though the price of wheat went down, from $5.00 a bushel to $2.46, the price of bread went up two cents. Why? Because a lot of the things related to the production of that loaf of bread went up—electrical rates, trucking rates, even the bag that the flour was in. But people make flour bags, you know, and some flour bag maker has got a job that he thinks is a good job.

MR. REAGAN: Also, there were 151 hidden taxes on that

finished loaf of bread, which accounted for more than half of its price.

MS. SHANAHAN: And on that dismal note, I'm afraid we have to call a halt.

SENATOR HUMPHREY: Oh, shucks. We were just getting along—

MS. SHANAHAN: Shucks, indeed. [Laughter and applause.]

I want to thank this remarkably distinguished and vigorous panel—Senator Hubert Humphrey of Minnesota, consumer advocate Ralph Nader, Harvard Professor of Economics Hendrik Houthakker, and former Governor Ronald Reagan of California—as well as our audience.

Thank you all, and good night. [Applause.]

Design: Pat Taylor

42156 144